Facts About the Leopard

By Lisa Strattin

© 2019 Lisa Strattin

Facts for Kids Picture Books by Lisa Strattin

Little Blue Penguin, Vol 92

Chipmunk, Vol 5

Frilled Lizard, Vol 39

Blue and Gold Macaw, Vol 13

Poison Dart Frogs, Vol 50

Blue Tarantula, Vol 115

African Elephants, Vol 8

Amur Leopard, Vol 89

Sabre Tooth Tiger, Vol 167

Baboon, Vol 174

Sign Up for New Release Emails Here

http://LisaStrattin.com/subscribe-here

Monthly Surprise Box

http://KidCraftsByLisa.com

All information in this book has been carefully researched and checked for factual accuracy. However, the author and publisher makes no warranty, express or implied, that the information contained herein is appropriate for every individual, situation or purpose and assume no responsibility for errors or omissions. The reader assumes the risk and full responsibility for all actions, and the author will not be held responsible for any loss or damage, whether consequential, incidental, special or otherwise, that may result from the information presented in this book.

All images are free for use or purchased from stock photo sites for commercial use.

Some coloring pages might be of the general species due to lack of available images.

I have relied on my own observations as well as many different sources for this book and I have done my best to check facts and give credit where it is due. In the event that any material is used without proper permission, please contact me so that the oversight can be corrected.

Contents

INTRODUCTION

The Leopard is a medium-sized wildcat that is natively found in different habitats across sub-Saharan Africa and in southern Asia. It is agile and opportunistic hunter that is able to exploit habitats that other big cats cannot because it spends a great deal of its time high up in the tree branches. There are seven different sub-species of Leopard which differ in appearance and habitat location. The African Leopard is the most common and widespread, the others are: the rare Amur Leopard, the Anatolian Leopard, the Barbary Leopard, the Sinai Leopard, the South Arabian Leopard and the Zanzibar Leopard. Although the African Leopard populations are doing well throughout much of their native range, some species are at risk with the Zanzibar Leopard is thought to be extinct, as of this writing.

Originally the leopard is thought to be a hybrid of the Lion and the Jaguar and has been the subject of a lot of genetic confusion and wasn't distinguished properly until just over 100 years ago. Some of this confusion is thought to be because of the Black Panther which is a Leopard with a completely black coat of fur, with some occasional faint markings.

Black Panthers tend to occur most in dense forests with the larger populations found in southern Asia than in Africa, and are born into a litter that also contains yellow cubs. Black Panthers are fairly common and it is thought that as many as 50% of the Leopards found living in the thick, tropical rainforests of the Malay Peninsula are black!

CHARACTERISTICS

The Leopard is a solitary and nocturnal hunter that hunts on the ground as well as in the trees. They are excellent climbers and spend the majority of the daytime hours lying in the shade of the branches in the trees or under a sheltered rock. They are different than other big cats, as they rely on being able to get close enough to prey before ambushing it, instead of a high speed chase.

Once caught and killed, they take their prey to safety, either into dense vegetation a couple of hundred meters away or up a tree trunk and into the branches before eating.

Leopards mark their territory with their scent and by making rough, rasping calls that are said to sound like the sawing of wood.

APPEARANCE

The Leopard has a long, slender body supported by short, stocky legs and a long tail that is used to maintain balance up in the trees. Leopards can vary greatly in color and markings, depending on their surrounding habitat. Those living on open grasslands have a light yellow background coat while those that live in forests are generally darker in color with more markings.

The dark, ring-like patterns that cover the Leopard are called rosettes, but these patterns become solid spots on the face and limbs (including rings on the tail) and give the big cat camouflage within the surrounding environment. They are incredibly strong and muscular and are able to pull themselves up trees using their legs and retractable claws, just like your housecat climbs trees. Their keen hearing and sight along with their long, sensitive whiskers, means that Leopards are also excellent night hunters.

LIFE STAGES

Throughout their natural range, Leopards have no specific breeding season, instead they are able to reproduce every couple of months. After a gestation period that lasts for around three months, the female gives birth to between 2 and 6 cubs in a litter, that are born blind and weigh just a pound or so.

Cubs are incredibly vulnerable in the wild and must remain hidden in dense vegetation until they are able to follow their mother around. This is between 6 and 8 weeks of age, camouflaged by their dark, woolly fur and blurry spots. They are weaned at around three months old, and remain with their mother for another 18 months until the mother is ready to mate again and then encourages her young to independently establish their own territories.

Although males are almost entirely solitary except when mating, females may not stray too far from their mother and many times will establish a home range that overlaps hers.

LIFE SPAN

Leopards tend to live for between ten and fifteen years in the wild, depending on the habitat and the food supply available.

SIZE

Adult Leopards are usually 40 to 70 inches long and weigh between 65 and 200 pounds.

HABITAT

Leopards are not only the widest ranging of all the big cats, but are actually one of the most adaptable and are found in a variety of different habitats. As previously stated, they are found throughout sub-Saharan Africa and southern Asia, but there are also small and isolated populations of them living in remote geographic locations in the Far East, Northern Africa and Arabia. The Leopard lives in a number of different areas as long as there is a good source of cover for protection and an ample supply of food including tropical rainforests, tree-lined savannah, barren deserts and mountain highlands. However, in some regions of their natural range their populations are threatened by the loss of their habitats to both deforestation and growing human settlements.

Home range sizes vary depending on the particular part of the world and the food available but the ranges of males are significantly larger than those of their female counterparts.

DIET

The Leopard is a silent and opportunistic hunter that only hunts and kills other animals in order to survive. They primarily hunt medium sized mammals like the deer and warthogs, that are often ambushed from the branches above or dense vegetation just meters away. They also eat a wide variety of small prey including birds, reptiles and rodents, even hunting Dung Beetles when larger animals are scarce.

By eating much smaller (and a wider variety) of prey, they are able to avoid the intense competition for food from other large carnivores like tigers and hyenas, which all share the native ranges. Leopards are incredibly strong and are capable of killing prey much heavier than themselves, such as antelopes, which are then hauled into the safety of the tree branches to be eaten immediately or saved for later.

FRIENDS AND ENEMIES

Generally the biggest threat to an adult Leopard is another leopard, along with the occasional lion or tiger that can get close enough to force a challenge. Young cubs are much more vulnerable which is why they remain hidden for the first few months of life. Leopard cubs are most at threat from hyenas, jackals, lions, tigers, snakes and Birds of Prey when they mother leaves them alone while she hunts for food.

SUITABILITY AS PETS

The leopard is not a good choice for a pet. They are a big cat that hunts for its prey and can kill animals much larger than themselves. You can watch a leopard in a zoo if you want to see one.

COLOR ME

COLOR ME

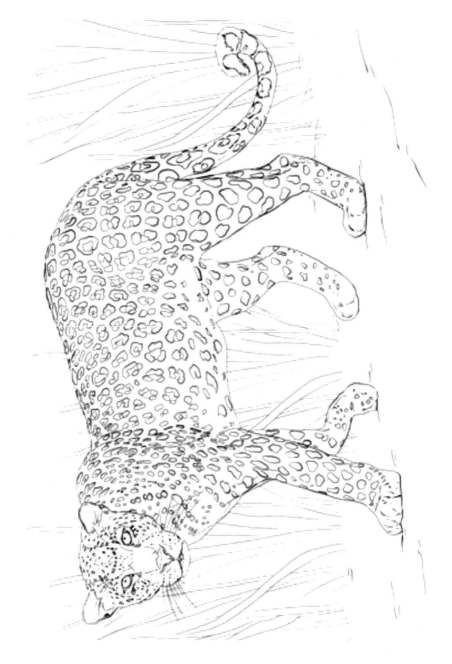

COLOR ME

COLOR ME

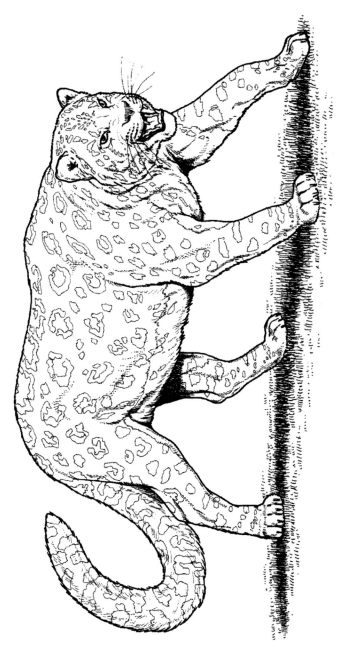

COLOR ME

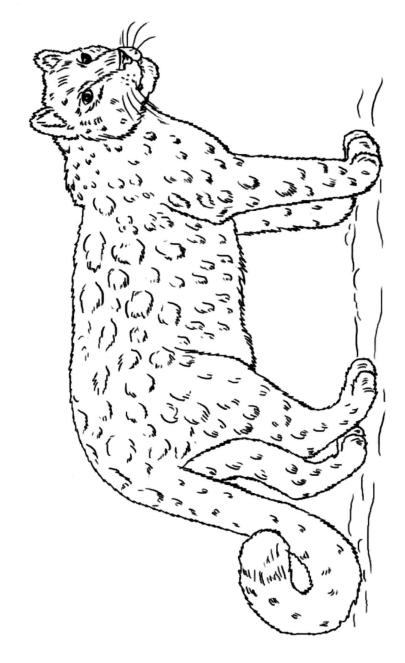

COLOR ME

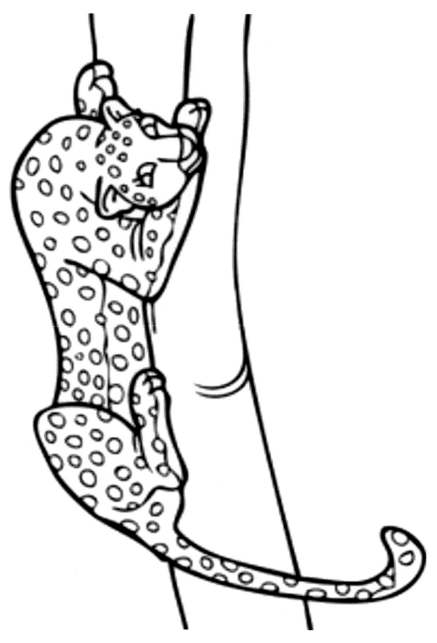

COLOR ME

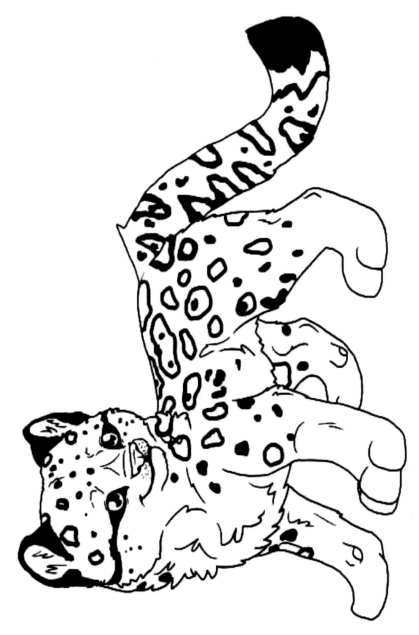

COLOR ME

Please leave me a review here:

http://lisastrattin.com/Review-Vol-207

For more Kindle Downloads Visit Lisa Strattin Author Page on Amazon Author Central

http://amazon.com/author/lisastrattin

To see upcoming titles, visit my website at LisaStrattin.com– all books available on kindle!

http://lisastrattin.com

PLUSH LEOPARD TOY

You can get one by copying and pasting this link into your browser:

http://lisastrattin.com/LeopardPlush

MONTHLY SURPRISE BOX

Get yours by copying and pasting this link into your browser

http://KidCraftsByLisa.com

Made in the USA
Monee, IL
30 July 2021

74447122R00024